Gentle
Marketing

How To Gently Attract Loads of New Customers!

CHALA DINCOY-FLAJNIK

I dedicate this book to my biggest cheerleader in all things and champion in especially this new chapter in my life – my wise, generous and opinionated

Mom

(Seni cok seviyorum Annecim!)

Chala Dincoy is the CEO and Founder of Coachtactics, *www.coachtactics.com.* She's a brand marketing expert who helps small businesses feel like a NATIONAL BRAND (without paying the big bucks!)

In her former life, Chala was an award winning marketer at companies such as Pepsi, Pizza Hut, Frito Lay, Diageo, Playtex and BIC Inc for 20 years. Now, she's an author, speaker and a certified business coach, who speaks about turning your brand into rocket fuel so you get more clients!

Chala dishes out big advice that's to the point, cuts your costs and helps make your brand look like a ROCK STAR to customers!

Contents

"It is not what we get. But who we become, what we contribute...that gives meaning to our lives."

Tony Robbins

1

Introduction

I have always hated my name while I was growing up. *"What the heck is a Chala?"* is what most people probably think when I introduce myself; if they even get that far.

Why were my parents so cruel, you ask? I think they really liked the name (which translates to a fruit turning into a nut in their language!) and didn't know any of the oncoming anguish to their teeny tiny bundle of joy.

Baby Chala (notice 70's couch behind me)

Born to Turkish immigrants in Montreal way too many years ago, I was the kid whose name was made fun of throughout school. I was the young adult who had trouble reserving cabs and often had to lie to the Starbucks lady who wanted to write my name on the cup. Throughout my life, I almost always had to repeat my name to someone when they first met me.

Little did I know that having the name Chala would be the cornerstone of making me a success as an entrepreneur. How could I guess that one day, having such a different and interesting name would set me apart and get people to remember me (whether in a good or bad way is debatable)?

Being memorable while being authentic and relevant makes people who need my help call ME instead of my competitors.

The other irony in my name Chala is the meaning. A fruit turning into a nut is nature's transition and a metaphor for how marketing works.

If you eat the fruit before it's turned into a nut, it tastes awful and is inedible. It's pretty much useless.

A "Chala" in Turkish, a green almond

Marketing is the same way, it takes time to develop into leads and grow your sales. If you try to cash in on your marketing too quickly-- in other words if your marketing isn't *Gentle*, then you can suffer some serious backlash from your potential clients and THAT is sure to leave a bad taste in your mouth!

If you don't have a funky name like me and still want to succeed in business, don't despair. This is a book where you'll learn how to market based on who you are and how you make others feel. It's a book that teaches you about effectively communicating how you can truly help people.

After marketing aggressively for big brands like Pepsi-Cole, Pizza Hut, Frito-Lay, Smirnoff and BIC Pens for 2 decades, I decided that there needed to be a game changer. I learned through experience that hard sell doesn't really work anymore, even for the big boys.

So I created a phenomenon that I call *Gentle Marketing*. A type of marketing even your **80 year old grandmother can use to sell something**. I've discovered as a business, when you concentrate on being good for others, you can ditch the fear, mistrust and distaste of the horrible beast called Marketing.

Read on to see what I really mean when I say "*Gentle Marketing*"

"The state of your life is nothing more than a reflection of the state of your mind."

Wayne Dyer

2

So What Is Gentle Marketing?

"*I'm sorry, I feel like you're attacking me with a sales pitch*" the lady said to me at my first ever networking meeting 8 years ago, tearing my heart and pride to shreds in seconds at the food buffet where we were chatting. This was in response to my attempt to introduce myself by coaching her on the spot (as I'd been trained in an intensive weekend coaching course to do) instead of telling her that I was a coach.

Yes, you read right.

I'd been taught that in order to get a coaching client, I was supposed to dive right into coaching someone to show them what it was that I did since most people wouldn't understand what coaching was according to the training.

Well, low and behold, the food buffet lady left her food and left the room after that unpleasant "attack" and needless to say, I soon followed her out the door.

As I drove home nearly in tears and in despair of ever getting a single client, my mind was reeling.

Here I was a 15 year veteran marketer for Fortune 500 companies like Pepsi Cola, Pizza Hut, Playtex and BIC Pens. I had managed millions of dollars and had to communicate with high level executives on a daily basis and I couldn't even get one person interested in my coaching at a lousy networking event.

How was I supposed to get a bloody client?

That same night, I had a Scarlett O'Hara-I'll-never-be-hungry-type of moment

I said to myself...

"Hey wait a second. You know what to do. Why don't you try to be yourself and just tell them HOW you help people instead of assuming they are interested in what you're selling?"

I decided to take everything I'd learned at my marketing jobs with the big brands and figure out a way to *Gentle* those techniques to be more effective and get myself some clients for my coaching practice. Now I help others to do the same.

I'm happy to say that since that fateful night, things have gone well...

- ☐ 7 years after this experience, I left my day job to launch my practice full time.

- ☐ I now work with my ideal clients making close to my BIC paycheque within only 1 year

- ☐ I have a coach that I pay $800/hour

- ☐ I get leads while I sleep

- ☐ I hired a team to support me

- ☐ I have a constant and steady flow of money

- ☐ I spend as much time with my son and family as I want

- ☐ I get up each and every day and love what I'm doing

I want the same things for you. It's not hard to be a *Gentle* marketer where people are attracted to your biz and want to buy from you.

The key elements of *Gentle Marketing* are:

1. Being very clear on what your distinct Brand Character is and ATTRACTING clients based on who you truly are at your core.

2. Having a very clear cohesive group of people that you've decided to help so that you can find them to market to.

3. Marketing ONE specific product or service that you can help clients with instead of saying that you can help them with EVERYTHING.

4. Developing a messaging based on their PAIN that will resound deeply with your target clients.

5. Finding and penetrating the world of your target clients with an attractive and *Gentle* message.

6. Putting together a cohesive plan to *Gently* attract the people who are dying for your help.

This book is a gentle guide and a gentle workbook.

I want you to sharpen your pencil and get ready to transform your marketing to one that works *gently* and effectively.   (And I'm using the word GENTLE a lot as I want you to breathe and realize this won't feel like a trip to the dentist)

"As you climb the ladder of success, check occasionally to make sure it is leaning against the right wall."

Anonymous

3

Bad Mistakes: Entrepreneurs In Attack Mode

On a recent Twitter Chat I co-hosted, I asked the question:
"How do you feel when someone's attacking you with their marketing?"

The responses were all unanimous; everyone hated it and ran from it.

Only mine was the compassionate suggestion...

"Maybe they don't know any better and don't have a good coach!"

Well, I could sympathize because I've certainly made mistakes where I was an entrepreneur in attack mode and I did it because I was trained to do it that way (see the previous chapter for the ugly story).

Here's a look at some others in attack mode:

Oily

A great example of an Attack Mode business is Oliver the Jewelry Buyer in Toronto. He has these really CHEESY TV ads about buying your 'gently used' jewelry. Even that term 'gently used' makes me laugh but back to dear Oliver, he's about 0 subtlety and all about cash. I mean he's nicknamed himself the "Cashman" for goodness sake.

On the other hand, one could argue that his very honesty and aggressiveness could in itself be an attraction to people who need and want his brand and business.

There's nothing *Gentle* about this guy, that's for sure.

Oliver the Jewelry Buyer

The Unsolicited

"Thank you for connecting with me on Twitter; here is my FREE eBook (PDF) about QR codes as my gift to you ..." is the type of automated message I often get when I follow someone on Twitter.

I rarely ever visit their Facebook page or their FREE e-book when I get this since those are a dime a dozen and I resent auto responders clogging up my inbox. It's not personalized, it's not about my pain and most of all it's not really all that *Gentle*.

Social Media isn't the only place that people are approaching their leads in unsolicited ways. I still have a duct cleaning company salesperson with a thick foreign accent call my home every other month. It usually takes a few seconds for me to hang up on them.

Why do businesses still do unsolicited and non-*Gentle* marketing?

Because once in a while it works.

I should know, as a teenager I had a summer job selling cemetery property.

My illustrious job was basically to make calls from our sophisticated lead list (the phone book) and to book a rep appointment with interested parties. I learned very quickly that death was not something people were willing to talk about over a cold call.

On the other hand, one funny old guy told me he didn't need cemetery services since he was going to be buried in his back yard. I hope he was joking!

I have to tell you though, I felt INTRUSIVE, DIRTY and REJECTED. This experience taught me that ATTACK marketing is neither a sustainable nor a desirable way to get business for my coaching practice.

Today, the *Gentle* approach where I reach out to help only when I see a need and speak in front of groups who are paying to hear me give them solutions to their pain gives me such a different feeling vs cold calling to sell cremations!

My Way Or The Highway Baby

Last night (fortuitous for this book) my husband Andy got an upsetting call from his gym owner where we've both been heavy duty members for 5 years.

Andy, who has muscles on even his ears, decided he needed a tougher workout and went to check out another gym. When his friends in class heard about the competitor, they also expressed interest in trying it out.

However, when a little sweaty bird told the owners of our gym what was happening, the owners went on hostile mode. The morning after they 'found him out'; they refused to answer Andy's "good morning" or to even glance at him when he twisted his ankle during a class and hobbled out!

Then the phone call came saying 'how dare you solicit business away from us!' As small business owners, we had supported and bragged about them to anyone who'd listen for over 5 years. I was appalled at their treatment of my darling. As a result, he isn't sure if he'll be staying with the gym and neither am I.

This really brought home the concept of *Gentle Marketing* for me. They were almost threatening him with the phone calls, accusing him of stealing business away, instead of trying to improve their offering in what they were doing so they could compete better with anyone in their market.

My hero author Wayne Dyer always says "Don't worry about other people's buildings or try to knock them down, instead focus on building your own as tall and as beautiful as you can".

That's just wonderful advice for any *Gentle Marketer*. Who cares what competitors are doing? As long as you're better and smarter and can help your clients more, why would you EVER worry about anyone leaving?

Leave Me Alone

I recently signed up for a webinar with a media guru and was literally BOMBARDED by automated follow up emails. I was automatically being almost threatened to sign up for the next step which was a whopping $6K investment! Email after email told me everything bad that would happen if I missed out on this amazing opportunity. Bombarding someone with anything, even love is not *Gentle*. It borders on stalking and that's not *Gentle Marketing*.

So don't make these bad entrepreneur attack mistakes. Be *Gentle*, be authentic and be attractive. You can buy SEO, you can buy advertising but you can't buy ATTRACTIVENESS. You just have to BE attractive. *Gently*.

"I had no idea that being your authentic self could make me as rich as I've become. If I had, I'd have done it a lot earlier."

Oprah

4

How to Brand Like A Celebrity So You Stop Getting Shopped On Price

Think fast! Who is a celebrity you admire (or drool over?) What types of products also make your heart race?

Powerful brands (like celebrities) last because they create a strong emotional connection between the person they are selling to, and the product or service themselves.

Every successful brand I've seen has a brand character. What is this thing? Basically, a brand character is a set of human traits associated with a certain product or service. (It's so much fun to do and can certainly help you to make more money in your business!)

You may be worried that you need BIG BUCKS to make this happen - NOPE (and more on that in a minute)

It all starts with the PERSON who represents the brand. Yes – this means you! A crucial ingredient of *Gentle Marketing* is being authentic and speaking in that brand voice that is true to who you are. Here are some examples:

Some ROCKING Brands

A brand's characteristics often reflect the founder's character, as in:

- **Richard Branson**: *Virgin* (the rebel with a cause)

Omg is that what I think it is?

- **Anita Roddick:** *Body Shop* (the social activist)

- **Oprah Winfrey:** The OWN Network (the philanthropist)

- **Donald Trump:***Trump Casino* (larger than life)

- **Howard Stern :** Radio Show Host (Shock jock)

Why Have A Brand Character In Your Biz?
If you want ...

- To attract customers by *GENTLE* means
- To stop getting SHOPPED ON PRICE
- To stop being CONFUSED WITH OTHER PEOPLE in your line of work
- Your tribe to REMEMBER you when they're in pain

Then you need a very clear and very memorable brand character for your business. When you attract people based on who you truly are, that's *Gentle Marketing*.

This applies to all businesses, even those that are working for multilevel marketing companies or banks or real estate offices.

Look below at how a lady who works in insurance set herself apart. Do you know any other insurance agent who cares about you like Mom does?

A Branding Success Story

Let me show you a great example of *Gentle Marketing* where a client developed a crystal clear brand character in her small business. My client Ann* (*name has been changed for confidentiality reasons) is a perfect example.

Ann had a small jewellery design business she was having difficulty growing.

When I asked her what the <u>human traits she wanted to associate</u> with her jewellery line were, she said:

1. funky
2. 40+ year old
3. successful
4. sexy
5. female

Her brand character was coincidentally the same as her target market.

What A Brand Character Is NOT

I want to make a distinction here. The brand character and the characteristics of a business's target customer **don't have to be the same.**

Take for example, the moving company **"Two Small Men with a Big Heart'.** Even though it's a small company, almost everyone I ask remembers seeing this company's name somewhere.

The **brand** character in this instance is:

1. Humorous
2. Generous
3. Male
4. Can lift heavy stuff.

It is apparent from the brand name itself. On the other hand, the characteristic of the **customer** target might be:

1. Female
2. 25-30years old
3. Wife of an executive
4. No interest in lifting the heavy stuff!

Do you see how different the brand characteristics can be from the target customer characteristics?

Ann's Celebrity

Back to Ann's *Gentle Marketing* story, when I asked her to actually visualize a celebrity who had the same characteristics as her jewellery line, she thought long and hard for weeks. After 3 weeks, she finally came up with the name **Susan Sarandon**, the Oscar winning actress, as the perfect representation of her brand character.

The Before And After Picture:

Prior to this exercise, this was Ann's business strategy:

1. <u>**Marketing vehicle**</u>: Ann had been using a blind (unaddressed) faxing service to mass fax black& white pictures of her work to offices in Toronto with zero returns. (egad) This is really not *Gentle Marketing*. It's unsolicited SPAM!

2. <u>**Packaging**</u>: She was using clear plastic bags to deliver the product to the customer.

3. <u>**Pricing**</u>: She'd been selling her jewellery at rock bottom prices. (great way to go broke)

4. **Distribution channel:** She would sell at any shop that would take her jewellery, namely mom and pop stores. (Smells like desperation to me)
5. **Brand name:** The name of Ann's jewellery line was– of course, called Ann Norton Designs since she thought all big designers used their own name on their line.

Once Ann locked in on the representation of her brand character of **Susan Sarandon**, she saw there was no **consistency between how she was conducting her business and what she wanted her product to stand for.**

This Is How Her Biz Strategy Changed:

1. **Marketing vehicle:** She invested in a stylish website and brochure. When you attract by virtue of who you are, that's *Gentle Marketing*.
2. **Packaging:** She promptly changed her packing to a polished mahogany box instead of the plastic bags.
3. **Pricing:** To absorb this increase in cost, as well as to reflect a higher quality, she increased her prices by 25%.
4. **Distribution channel:** She only targeted high end stores to sell her line. The mom and pops could no longer afford her goods anyway.

5. **Brand name**: Perhaps the biggest benefit of having crystallized her brand character was that the name of her brand became a more fitting and descriptive '**Timeless**'(not her real company name)

Armed with these changes, **Timeless** has grown into a successful brand that is now ONLY SOLD at exclusive boutiques and online.

Ann no longer wonders what colour to use on her business cards and what her pricing strategy should be. She's a *Gentle Marketer*. She just asks herself the question 'what would Susan Sarandon say, do, be seen in or price herself at?' and the roadmap to her business strategy is clear.

Hate Celebs?

Don't feel attached to the actual celebrity to be a *Gentle Marketer*; everyone has a different vision of what celebrity's characteristics are.

Most important in this exercise, is that you define the actual characteristics of your brand as any human and make sure you consistently act that way through all aspects of your business strategy. You can use your Aunt Mabel for all I care as long as your predominant brand characteristic is clear and concise and holds your communication plan consistent.

How To Create A Brand Character That Attracts Your Dream Clients!

1. Think of the top 3 human traits you have that people know about you.
2. Think of a celebrity who reflects that.
3. What are your top 3 characteristics?
4. What celebrity comes to mind?
5. Do these reflect the celebrity
   - Your brand name
   - Your website
   - Your pricing
   - How/where you get clients
   - Your keynote title
   - Your blogs/eBooks writing style
   - Your social media presence

How Do I Use This In My Biz? (Some brilliant examples)

Suzanne Evans

Here's how one of my fave coaches Suzanne Evans is using it. She's ballsy; she's in your face and doesn't apologize for it. On herwebsite she actually proclaims it. This lady swears like a sailor on stage at her events and sells t-shirts with 'Hell Ya' on the back. She also sells stuffed toy grenades with the letter 'F' written on them. She throws them into the audience and says she's throwing 'F bombs'. She is distinct, different and she's got droves of clients. Here's who I think her celebrity is: Gordon Ramsey, a British chef with a potty mouth.

Gordon Ramsev

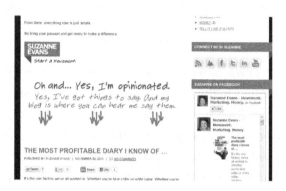

Patagonia

Another one I love is the clothing retail giant Patagonia's brand character. I got this email on Cyber Monday, the highest online shopping traffic day of the year. I think their brand character is the famed Canadian Environmentalist David Suzuki.

David Suzuki

When I scrolled down, here's what they had to say

Today is Cyber Monday. It will likely be the biggest online shopping day ever. Cyber Monday was created by the National Retail Federation in 2005 to focus media and public attention on online shopping. But Cyber Monday, and the culture of consumption it reflects, puts the economy of natural systems that support all life firmly in the red. We're now using the resources of one-and-a-half planets on our one and only planet.

Because Patagonia wants to be in business for a good long time – and leave a world inhabitable for our kids – we want to do the opposite of every other business today. We ask you to buy less and to reflect before you spend a dime on this jacket or anything else.

REDUCE
WE make useful gear

What kind of email should you be sending to your clients that will **underscore your brand character and differentiate you in the minds of your target consumers?** Authenticity is *Gentle Marketing*.

Chala Dincoy (that`s me!)

Here's one from my brand character. My brand character celebrity is a journalist by the name of Lisa Ling (not to be confused with the butt-kicking Charlie's Angel).

Lisa Ling

To me, she stands for professionalism with an edge. She can often be found in prisons or sex clubs doing exposes. I myself recently posted a blog called "What I learned about marketing from a naughty spam".

A former colleague said she found it offensive and asked if I'd had a huge unsubscribe rate. The truth is I think it's an interesting way to look at marketing and my direct but fun approach didn't see anything wrong with using a naughty spam to illustrate my teachings about effective marketing.

In fact, I got one of the highest open rates of the year with this newsletter and no more than the usual unsubscribes. Most of all, it sent my message about my brand character which I also reinforce in my keynotes, website and social media posts.

What celebrity lies at the heart of your business and more importantly—how are you using it to be different, to stay memorable and to get more clients?

Will Your Personality Attract Clients?

"Chala, Chala, Chala!" my boss shook his head as he sighed in disappointment at my questionable joke during a meeting with one of our suppliers. The poor man was fond of me and he was also used to me but as he'd disclosed at my recent performance review, he didn't think I had "corporate maturity". That folks, was my first ever job exactly 20 years ago. (Hmmm – he was probably right.)

The Subterfuge

But I went too far with his advice. Sad to say, through the years, I shed my jokes, my laughter and my sense of fun to climb up the corporate ladder. I can't say that I was all too good at the subterfuge because I never quite fit in until I found my last job. At my last job, I was too old, too experienced and too good at what I did to care much about "corporate maturity". I was also surrounded by a warm, caring and appreciative culture. The honeymoon lasted 7 long years and it prepared me to fly out on my own.

The Entrepreneur Personality

Now as an entrepreneur and a *Gentle Marketer*, my personality is the most critical element of my marketing. My flippant jokes and irreverent style are the key things that set me apart from hundreds of other marketing coaches. As a small business owner, are you trying to fit an "acceptable" mold or owning who you truly are at your heart?

Too scared to be me

When you think and talk in a way that you think is "acceptable" to your boss, your clients, your networks or your newsletter audience, you're actually cheating. You're cheating yourself out of living authentically and cheating others by fooling them into thinking that you're a match for them when in reality, the people you're too scared to attract probably need you the most.

Will the Real Slim Shady Please Stand Up?

As in Eminem song which definitely dates me, will you let the real you please stand up and stop thinking about whether it's acceptable or not?

The fake allegedly "acceptable" you is uncomfortable, unsustainable and a waste of your true shining self. So kudos to the "unacceptable" you and feel the joy of attracting those who love you for your courage and spirit and will pay big bucks for your honesty because you are DIFFERENT than others who are all so very "acceptable".

As a *Gentle* Marketer, YOUR character is your number one tool in your toolkit. Why not use it to differentiate yourself and attract loads of new clients? Life is too short to be living from someone else's perspective for you.

If you don't use this, nothing you do will be as effective in gaining new clients.

Workbook

1. What are the top 3 words that people who first meet you describe you as? (ie. Sweet, sensible, intelligent, shy?)

    _____

    _____

    _____

    _____

    _____

    _____

2. What is different about you as a person (ie. Your afro, your 6 kids, your off the wall sense of humour?)

    _____

    _____

    _____

    _____

_____

_____

_____

3.   Who is a celebrity who fits the above description?
     (ie. Donald Trump, Oprah, Gandhi etc?)

_____

_____

_____

_____

_____

_____

4.   Where can you reflect this Brand Character/Brand
     Voice? (your tagline, business card, web copy,
     blogs)

_____

_____

_____

_____

_____

_____

_____

5.   What changes are you willing to do to your
     marketing collateral now to have a consistent and
     distinct Brand Voice so that you can become more
     memorable? (change any of the above in Q4.)

_____

_____

_____

_____

_____

_____

_____

"I don't know the key to success but the key to failure is to try to please everyone."
Bill Cosby

Bullseye: How To Target Your Best Customers

"What exactly is IT that you do?"

That age old question small business owners encounter is really at the crux of a lot of my clients' key business issues. They have *no clarity* around what specific product or service best represents what they actually do or sell.

Some people are so conflicted about which product or service to focus on that incredibly, they've built two separate businesses, complete with multiple business cards, and even some with multiple websites.

Imagine the energy of maintaining two separate businesses. No wonder the first step of any coaching relationship is to achieve clarity of objectives.

Why do people do this, you ask?

- Is it because they love joining 3 different types of associations and thrive on meeting strangers every day?
- Is it because they feel the warm glow of joy working long hours trying to meet different industry needs?
- Or is it because they are just plain scared that if they define their product or service too narrowly, they won't have enough business to survive on?

I personally find it so sad and frustrating when clients simply cannot choose what business they're in.

Knowing who you help and how you help them is a big part of *Gentle Marketing*. If you try to help everyone and do everything with them, you will find that it's confusing for you and for your audience. It's also ineffective and inefficient.

So I devised a simple method to help demonstrate the importance of picking just one type of CLIENT and one THING YOU SELL to base your communication model on.

Imagine 4 different types of business models.

1. The Generalist
2. The Client Specialist
3. The Thing They Sell Specialist
4. The Perfectly Niched

The Generalist:

I'll demonstrate these models using restaurants.

The **first** being: **Applebee's**

Applebee's menu

At Applebee's, the CLIENT TYPE could be business people, families with small children, teenagers. Anyone and everyone.

Similarly, the Applebee's THINGS THEY SELL are Mexican cuisine, French cuisine, American cuisine and any other type of cuisine that you can imagine, I'm sure.

Now what kind of pricing does Applebee's have? It's a pretty affordable restaurant. It's for everyone, after all. Also, what kind of food quality does the encyclopaedia type menu at Applebee's feature? Let's just say it's not the kind of place you'd wish your boyfriend would propose at.

This is the type of business that caters to every CLIENT TYPE and features EVERYTHING TO SELL. It's not niched at all...that's why I call them the *Generalist*.

The Thing They Sell Specialist: The **second** restaurant type I want you to consider

is **Starbucks**.

They cater to every type of CLIENT TYPE from business people to families, similar to Applebee's. What's different about them is their focus on THING THEY SELL and that's all about coffee. Now, I know they sell muffins and even sandwiches but the crux of their business and their communication is coffee. Why else would employees be called Baristas?

Because Starbucks are experts in coffee, they actually can charge a premium for their expertise but because they cater to EVERY CLIENT TYPE, they're still not as narrowly niched as other businesses. This is the *Thing They Sell Specialist* type of business model.

The Client Specialist: The **third** restaurant type I want you to consider is **Chuck E. Cheese's.**

In this business model which I've called the *Client Specialist*, things are flipped from the Starbucks Model. Chuck E. Cheese's has only 1 CLIENT TYPE, families with young children but THINGS THEY SELL are varied. I hope you're getting an idea by now of where this niching model is going.

The Perfectly Niched: The last and IDEAL model of business for niching is demonstrated by the **fourth** restaurant type and that's a local snazzy French restaurant called **Auberge Du Pommiers.**

The menu is very short. The clientele are high rollers. The food is famously to die for. They only do French cuisine and mostly cater to the wealthy Toronto downtown businessmen. I once got a gift certificate for $100 to eat there and it wasn't even enough to cover our appetizers! (But damn – they were good appetizers!)

They only have 1 CLIENT TYPE, business people and SELL ONLY 1 type of thing, French food.

I want you to consider moving your business model from an Applebee's to an Auberge. There are many reasons for this which I will go into in detail.

Even if you could move yourself from a Generalist to any kind of specialist, you'll be better off than you are right now.

Here's a chart that sums up the Niching Models

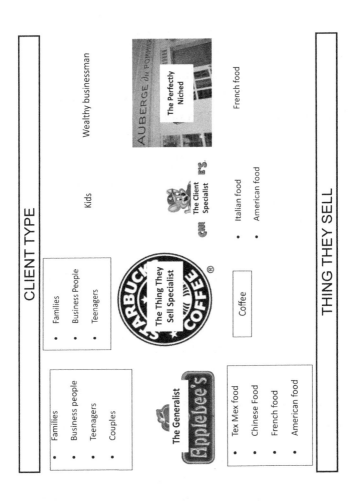

How do you pick?

That is the big question isn't?

Part of *Gentle* Marketing is knowing who you help and how you help them. Here's a real simple way to decide for once and for all what your exact niche is.

The process is simple but implementing the process takes a lot of market research. I.e. Talking to potential clients in those niches and talking to anyone and everyone who are currently earning a living in those niches. For example, before choosing my niche of Marketing to Entrepreneurs, I spoke to literally over a hundred coaches and consultants.

Let me take you through the process of picking your niche.

Step 1: Make a list of all the different CLIENT TYPES you've ever worked or considered working with.

Step 2: Make a list of all the possible product or services that you can sell (THINGS YOU SELL)

Step 3: For each CLIENT TYPE and THINGS YOU SELL combo, give yourself a score out of 1 to 10, 10 being the most desirable for you. Rate the following criteria:

  a) **Fit for you**—your personal preference, skill set, experience and background
  b) **Fit for the income you want**—how many of this group x how much price you would charge per person

c) **Access**—your ability to reach your target and how accessible they are to you in large numbers

Example

Here's the exercise I actually went through for my own business

1. **Fit for your personality, skill set, experience, background and preference**

- Leadership coaching to CEOs: Score 8/10
- Marketing to entrepreneurs: Score 10/10

2. **Ability to generate the revenue you want**

- Leadership coaching to CEOs: Score 10/10
- Marketing to entrepreneurs: Score 8/10

3. **Access**

- Leadership coaching to CEOs: Score 2/10 (I didn't know or know anyone who knew a single CEO, they were difficult to reach for me)
- Marketing to entrepreneurs: Score 10/10

Total Scores

- **Leadership coaching to CEOs: 20**
- **Marketing to entrepreneurs: 28**

I guess by now you know that I teach marketing to entrepreneurs and have been very successful with my niche. I'm living proof that this stupefying simple way to pick your niche works!

You too can do this simple exercise and move on towards the light where your *Gentle* marketing plan and consequently more clients await.

Top Reasons Why You're Insane If You Don't Niche

You're an expert baby!

When my munchkin refused to graduate from pureed food to solids, (stubborn like his momma!) I went out and found every paediatric nutritionist in North America. After going through 3 of them, I finally landed on one who was an EXPERT in transitioning to solids. Think that's crazy? I agree but we were desperate and I was looking for an EXPERT. I would've done anything to get some educated help.

When your business is niched very finely and you're always talking about and writing about and consulting about the same PAIN point. You then become regarded as an EXPERT and you'll see why that's not just bragging rights but good for your business.

Gentle Marketers are EXPERTS in their field. They are sought out and revered.

Get Paid More!

How much do you think I was willing to pay this paediatric nutritionist who actually got my baby to start eating again? I paid her around 10% more than what other nutritionists were charging per hour but I'll be honest and tell you I would have paid her DOUBLE that, just to stop my son from starving. That's what happens when you're perceived as an expert who knows how to solve a client's very specific pain.

Niching is the *Gentlest* way to command a higher fee.

Once you're perceived to be the only right person for that specific job, nobody will even blink at or haggle about your prices ever again.

No More Competition!

When I ask my clients to do some research about their niche by calling their competition, they are appalled and surprised.

"Why would anyone help me take business away from them by giving me information?"

When you pick a niche that's distinctly different than theirs, you're no longer the enemy who'll take money out of their pockets. Instead you become the person they can refer others to.

This happens in coaching all the time; I refer many clients to Relationship Coaches or Lifestyle Coaches. Similarly, they refer to me their entrepreneur clients who are in need of marketing help.

Gentle Marketers are natural collaborators. They refer others in the same industry who are slightly different than they are because they can afford to do so if they're very specific about who they help and what they do.

Higher Quality Clients

People who are looking for experts are aware that experts are different than people who deal in all things.

When you increase the quality of what you offer in terms of value (and experts offer more value) the **clients you attract will be of the same quality.**

It's the law of attraction. You are what you attract.

One of my most successful clients has recently changed the way she does business to reflect her niche better. Alana (not her real name) had an ad agency where she serviced technology clients, food service clients and retails clients. The only thing they had in common was that they needed her design services.

Once she did the exercise to niche properly on food service clients and decided to offer them Inbound Marketing services as her specialty, she was Perfectly Niched. Remember, a *Gentle* Marketer is attractive by virtue of their clarity on WHO they help and WHAT they help them with.

Not only did Alana get more clients but she got higher revenues per client versus a year ago. She credits becoming more focused around her niche with her double digit growth.

Easy Peasy Marketing Decisions

So let's say you have two products you want to market.

Which one do you talk about first on your website?

When you serve two target markets, whose trade show do you invest the very limited marketing funds you have for this year?

These are very real questions that small businesses face and it's exhausting. There aren't enough hours in the day, or money in the bank for any business to be able to afford to have a multitude of products, services as well as target markets to wow. Picking one or two just makes economic sense.

You'll find out more on how to easily decide on where to spend your *Gentle* Marketing time and money in the Chapter <u>Where To Find Clients So You Can Mesmerize Them.</u>

Carve out 'Mind Real-Estate'

When you're always in your niche customers' world and you're always talking about the same thing, it is a natural process that they begin to get to know you.

In brand marketing, there's something called 'mind real estate'. This is how brands carve out a space in the mind of their consumer. That's what picking a narrow niche does, you begin to start immediately coming to their minds when the need for your specific product or service arises. For example, when you're always at the same association meetings as your potential clients or you're featured as a speaker at their industry conference, people start to get to know you.

My clients and I have a *Gentle* Marketing Plan where we're always present where our potential clients are with the same messaging that says we can help with their pain.

Now, some clients report that only a few months of being where their clients are has resulted in seeing the same sunny faces and actually starting to make friends with their target market. Imagine that!

Get Results Pronto!

Want clients yesterday? You're not alone.

If you're a small business you have no time for elaborate promotions and events that are planned 3 months down the line to get results. When you niche finely, you can stop flying by the seat of your pants and going on gut feeling to decide where you should be marketing. Having a niche allows you to make a more formalized annual marketing plan, full of details of where and when to find your niche target and how to most effectively reach them. OOPS – you don't HAVE a marketing plan?

No worries – more on that later!

Gentle Marketing takes the panic out of your attempts to get a client. A niche allows you to have a clear plan, which allows you to attract clients much faster than you would if you were going in every direction;

trying every new marketing tactic and looking like a wild woman.

Referrals Referrals!

Gentle Marketing is allowing other people to rave about you to people who need your help. When people can refer you as the 'guy who coaches consultants to get to a million dollar client base' that's a MUCH STRONGER testimonial than ...

'I know a guy who does some business development work'.

If you're having trouble deciding what exactly it is that you do or sell, how do you expect your peers to understand it or better yet, to describe it to others?

People talk about what they understand. They steer clear of what confuses them. Give them the clarity and you'll be rewarded with more referrals.

Getting referrals is such a big part of *Gentle* Marketing that it deserves its own chapter. For more on that, check out the Chapter8 Getting Ravers To Refer You

Niche-Phobia

So now that you know you NEED to choose a defined target customer to be a *Gentle* Marketer, are you experiencing High Anxiety when you think about picking a Niche?

What exactly is Niche-Phobia, you ask?

It's when you start sweating from every orifice once someone tells you that to get more clients, you need to market to one specific client group (e.g. overworked IT professionals) and offer only one product or service (e.g. Work-life balance coaching).

Sound familiar?

The concept of niching is very well-known and highly touted by not just but by all business and marketing experts.

So why is it that I run across Niche-Phobia (coined so cleverly by a very smart client of mine this week) as almost the biggest problem of start-ups?

Here are some Myths on Niching...

Myth #1: I Can't Do This Because I Sell More Than One Thing

My client Nancy was a sales rep at a community newspaper. She had a quota to sell 35 different products ranging from regular ad space to sponsorships to special events. Do you think she took kindly to being told to pick only one type of customer to target and to speak about only 1 of those 35 products as our first step to getting her more clients? She thought I was crazy!

Soon enough, she found out for herself that confused minds don't buy. When she niched herself properly and in a few months became known as the go-to gal for car dealerships in Oakville to run special promotions on-line, she found her sales going up for ALL of her 35 products.

Myth #2: I'm No Expert!

Richard, a highly intelligent owner of an ad agency refused to pick a niche even though he was keenly interested in the environment and knew of ways that his business could offer green products. I was thrilled with the discovery of his hobby because Richard clearly knew so much about and had such a passion for everything recycled.

Richard wasn't so sure however, no matter how long we discussed it and how much we talked about how to close his perceived gap to become an 'expert' in the environmental niche, he never felt good enough to call himself a 'green' ad agency.

Years later after we'd ended our work together; I got a delighted call from Richard. After all that time rejecting to niche in a green positioning, because of a few things we'd changed on his website and his own lifelong involvement in all things green, Richard got a job! He had been hired by an environmental paper company as a brand ambassador based on their belief that he was an expert in the field!

I had to laugh at that one. Life is funny indeed and niching works!

Myth #3: I Will Starve

You may be worrying that if you choose only 1 target group and 1 type of service or product sale of that single target group won't pay the bills. This just isn't so.

Picking specifically WHAT TYPE of people you will be helping will REDUCE your confusion and INCREASE the effectiveness of your marketing.

Do you have the resources or even the energy to invest in 2 different industry trade shows?

Are you strong enough to network with several different professions consistently and simultaneously so that they'll get to know, like and trust you?

The truth is without a clear decision on who you help and what you offer, you'll end up confusing your audience. Remember, a confused audience doesn't buy.

Someone who is crystal clear on who they help and what they do to help will be much more attractive to your competitor who did bite the bullet and made the tough decision on how to niche.

I'm not saying you can't sell more than just 1 thing to more than 1 group of people.

I'm suggesting you pick 1 of each to start with and just get out there.

After all, if you don't know who specifically you want to sell to, how will you know where to go to find them?

Light at the end of the tunnel

I've been teaching my clients to niche for a good decade.

Ironically, I only felt Niche-Phobia once I left my day job and launched my business full-time. I found myself paralysed by indecision about whether I should pursue Leadership coaching or Brand Coaching. I was equally qualified and passionate about both niches. After doing 15 talks to hundreds of people about Leadership over several months, I found to my astonishment that all the clients I was getting were for Brand Coaching regardless of how or why they met me.

My niche found me!

Now as I speak and market to small business owners in helping them to brand their businesses, my only advice is don't let niche-phobia paralyse you. Regardless of what you do or who you serve, get out there and get what I call "Human Face Time" meaning network, meet old colleagues for coffee and tell them a few things you can offer. Speak at any association about anything you're passionate about and sooner or later I promise, your niche will find you.

I only hope I can convince you to do it sooner!

Workbook

1. What are at least 3 different target groups (CLIENT TYPE) you'd like to work with?

    _____

    _____

    _____

    _____

    _____

2. What are at least 3 different products or services (THING YOU SELL) that you can sell to your target group?

    _____

    _____

    _____

    _____

    _____

3. Rate each permutation of CLIENT TYPE-THING YOU SELL COMBO on a scale of 1-10 for:

    o   Fit for your personality, skill set, experience, background and preference

    o   Ability to make generate the revenue you want

    o   Access

    _____

    _____

    _____

    _____

    _____

    _____

4. Add the scores for each permutation of possible CLIENT TYPE-THING YOU SELL

    _____

    _____

    _____

    _____

    _____

    _____

5.   Which is the highest score?

_____

_____

_____

_____

_____

_____

"The single biggest problem in communication is the illusion that it has taken place."

George Bernard Shaw

6

Made You Look! What To Say To Your Clients To Get Them To Throw Their Credit Cards At You

Say What?

Developing your marketing message is such a critical part of *Gentle* Marketing that if you do everything right but get this one element wrong, you'll confuse your audience and find yourself floundering in every direction but the right one.

Here are the steps to build the right *Gentle* message:

Who's hearing it anyway?

The first rule of any marketing is to know WHO you're aiming your message at.

If you don't know or can't pinpoint a single large group of similar minded people, then you can't build an effective message for them.

So stop telling people in your elevator speech (the short introduction you do at business meetings) that you work with *everyone* and start narrowing down a group of people who have a reason for being together (ie. Entrepreneurs, dentists, new moms, realtors etc.)

Don't Assume My Pain

Basing your message on your target client's pain is how you get attention from them *Gently* and without even trying.

It's a spot on strategy.

One warning though—what if the pain YOU THINK they have is different from what THEY THINK?

An example of an assumption disaster was when I was actually the client. An ad agency who was trying to sell me an ad campaign based on increasing our brand awareness when I was a brand manager at a popular consumer goods company did a great job frustrating me.

The agency had created an elaborate campaign strategy with detailed examples of execution. Not once had they asked me or checked their assumption that our brand awareness was a marketing issue we wanted to spend money on. Little did they know that the brand enjoys a whopping 99% brand awareness in Canada.

After 2 hours of this presentation droning on, I had to finally pipe up and tell them that our brand pain wasn't really about awareness but that it was a *quality perception issue* with our key target segment.

That really set the agency on their ears and made us choose not to work with them. If they didn't listen to us even before the first date, what kind of marriage would we have?

Same goes for you and your clients.

A *Gentle* Marketer doesn't assume their client's pain. They make sure they speak to enough potential clients to understand exactly what that common pain is, and then they develop a messaging and a strategy to help them address it.

Change Me Over

As a client in pain, I'm interested in **how you can help me**—but even more important than that, I'm interested in **how you're going to change my life and my business**. This transformation piece is really key in how you convince people to work with you.

Here's my elevator pitch that speaks to this—

"I help overwhelmed and exhausted entrepreneurs make a marketing plan to get new clients"

That's the transformation-taking clients from presumably no clients to filling their practice.

From The Elevator To The Net

Your message is so important that it's the one thing that is consistent between your elevator pitch to your website copy to your keynote title to your blog content. It needs to be on everything!

It's the same captivating transformation message you broadcast on all frequencies and channels 24/7 constantly.

Figure out the right messaging—talk in their words about your client's pain and how you transform lives and you'll become a marketing gold medal winner who will attract clients like cheesecake to PMS'ers.

Now go ahead and do your homework questions below and let's really get to the heart of the matter!

Workbook

1. What are your ideal client's top 3 pain points that you can help them with?

_____

_____

_____

_____

_____

_____

2. How certain are you of these pain points being the most relevant for your clients? Do you need to check your assumptions with them?

_____

_____

_____

_____

_____

_____

3. What is the transformation that you bring as a result of working together? (ie. I help my clients get at least 1 new client a month)

_____

_____

_____

_____

_____

_____

4. What is your elevator pitch (your intro statement) that reflects this transformation?

_____

_____

_____

_____

_____

_____

5. What will you change in your marketing as a result of reflecting this transformational message more prominently? (web copy, biz card?)

_____

_____

_____

_____

_____

_____

6. What would be the title of a blog you'd write to convey your transformational messaging?

_____

_____

_____

_____

_____

_____

"People rarely succeed unless they have fun in what they are doing."

Dale Carnegie

7

Where To Find Your Clients So You Can Mesmerize Them

Hang Out With Your Future Clients

"Chala if it weren't for our work together, I'd never in a million years be presenting at this trade show" said my client Mandy (not her real name).

That's precisely the kind of result that I want you to have after going through the exercise of getting into your clients' world below.

First Step Reminder: Get Narrow

Remember this exercise works most effectively when you've chosen a very narrow target group as your niche. The best way to narrow your niche is to pick a vertical industry if possible to focus on--such as realtors, project managers or nurses. This is the most crucial step in starting to get into your clients' world.

Step 2: Map Out Where They Hang Out

All day, every day your potential clients are hanging out somewhere. They are also in pain.

As a *Gentle* Marketer, if you've done a good job niching and have picked a cohesive group of people to target, they are most likely hanging out together. That's where you need to be, my friend!

The whole idea about *Gently* surrounding your target clients is so that you can intercept them and expose them to your message that you understand their pain and can most definitely help them. I had to laugh about Gently stalking anyone but that's exactly what I want you to do.

Figure out where to run into your niche of clients and then in a variety of ways, tell them that you help other people with pain similar to theirs and that you can also help them.

Simple as apple pie!

Here are 6 categories of gentle strategies to intercept your target.

1. *Lifestyle*

A lot of your clients do this or are like this. For example, if your target group is environmentally friendly dads, a lot of them probably drive a Prius.

> Possible Marketing Action: Run a Face book campaign for Prius owners.

Another example of how to use Lifestyle to market is if you target healthy and wealthy boomers as one of my clients does. Here's what we came up with for her.

> Possible Marketing Action: Join their lawn and tennis club and sponsor one of their galas. Alternately, she's also gotten into speak at the Granite Club to reach them. This is an exclusive membership only club where they socialize. This is their lifestyle and she's reaching them through marketing in their world.

2. *Media*

One of the most important ways to intercept your target is to find out what media (including online) your target client group consumes. What social media do they use, which LinkedIn groups are they in, which publications and electronic media do they regularly follow?

Possible Marketing Action: Write an article in the *Choice* magazine for coaches

Possible Marketing Action: Frequently comment on the *Small Business Toronto* Linked in group discussion threads.

3. *Association/Organization*

This is where the rubber of whether you've picked a good niche meets the road of whether you can find your target client group in a cohesive association or organization. For example, my financial broker client couldn't find as many association meetings to attend when his target was 'small to medium sized businesses'. However, once he niched down to the gifting industry, his entire marketing calendar was revealed to him in an instant.

Possible Marketing Action: Speak at the AIC (Association of Independent Consultants) about how consultants can close clients faster.

Possible Marketing Action: Become a member and go to all meetings of the POC (Professional Organizers of Canada) if your target group is organizers.

4. *Meetings/Conferences/Trade Shows/Events*

Your target market is even right now, probably at some type of trade meeting, conference, event or trade show and if you haven't planned to be there, you may not even know about it. There are so many conferences in any given city that there are websites dedicated to just tracking them. (example: *www.conferencealerts.com* or *www.allconferences.com*)

Another tool I use is to set up a free Google alert for keywords such as 'entrepreneur conference' or 'entrepreneur trade show'. Set one up for who you target.

Every time there's an event planned or anything online appears, I get a Google alert email with the info. It was because of this very alert that I pitched the idea of setting up a Coach's Corner where I coached individuals throughout the conference and elevated my profile to the thousands of recipients of the newsletter and media that the SOHO SME Entrepreneurs' Event got.

Get on it and you too can plan to be part of your target's world!

> Possible Marketing Action: Become a vendor at a Real Estate trade show.

5. *Other Professionals*

What other businesses sell products and services to your target client?

What kind of joint venture or cross referral deals can you set up to reach your target?

> Possible Marketing Action: If you're a marketing Virtual Assistant and your target clients are accountants, you can joint venture with a lawyer who often works with

them so he/she will refer you and you'll refer them. You can even set up a fee structure to compensate each other for referrals.

6. *Your Competition*

If you've niched properly, you don't truly have competition.

Either you serve a different part of the market need (you're a branding coach vs. a money coach) or you serve a different type of person (you help boomers who've left corporate careers or you help young mompreneurs) which is why you have no true competition. Now your job is to find others like you and band together to make a bigger impact and reach your target in a more meaningful way.

Possible Marketing Action:

I put together a 'Coach's Buffet' of 6 different coaches of different disciplines who could help young women entrepreneurs at the Toronto Women's Expo. The different coaches featured were experts in branding, money, mindset, stress, and health. I sold this idea to several conferences in exchange for phenomenal exposure and selling opportunities for all of us at the show.

Step 3: Plan it

The next step is for you to form your own Map of where your future clients are hanging out.

An example of my marketing with other coaches

Follow the questions below to see how. Remember this IS your marketing plan. It is how you will be spending your time and money on. Get specific, do your research and come up with a solid plan to grow your business.

Workbook

1. Who is the target group that's in the middle of your Map of Where Your Future Clients Hang Out?

_____

_____

_____

_____

_____

2. What is a Possible Marketing Action you can do in the *Lifestyle* section? Add specifics including budget and timing please. You will be entering this info in your 2013 plans.

_____

_____

_____

_____

_____

_____

3. What is a Possible Marketing Action you can do in the *Media* section? Add specifics including budget and timing please. You will be entering this info in your 2013 plans.

_____

_____

_____

_____

_____

_____

4. What is a Possible Marketing Action you can do in the *Association/Organization* section? Add specifics including budget and timing please. You will be entering this info in your 2013 plans.

_____

_____

_____

_____

_____

_____

5. What is a Possible Marketing Action you can do in the *Meetings/Conferences/Trade Shows/Events* section? Add specifics including budget and timing please. You will be entering this info in your 2013 plans.

_____

_____

_____

_____

_____

_____

6. What is a Possible Marketing Action you can do in the *Other Professionals* section? Add specifics including budget and timing please. You will be entering this info in your annual plans.

_____

_____

_____

_____

_____

_____

7. What is a Possible Marketing Action you can do in the *Your Competition* section? Add specifics including budget and timing please. You will be entering this info in your annual plans.

_____

_____

_____

_____

_____

_____

"Friendship is a single soul dwelling in two bodies."

Aristotle

8

Getting Ravers To Refer You

The *Gentlest* Marketing is letting others do it for you. I don't mean hiring sales reps although you could easily do that and teach them a thing or two about *Gentle* Marketing. No, I'm talking about getting enough buzz and enough raving fans to actually start getting you clients without you lifting a digit.

Here are some ways to generate *Gentle* referrals.

Who's In The Bag?

The biggest sources of referrals are your existing clients, the ones who are already "in the bag" so to speak. They think you're the cat's meow because helloooooooooo-they're already working with you! If you're as fabulous as you should be (because remember, you're an EXPERT at what you do since you're finely niched in your subject matter) then your clients should be soaring and succeeding through their challenges.

Their success is a cause for celebration and what **better way to celebrate** than to suggest they tell others about how well they're doing?

Brag Much?

If you brag about yourself, shame on you, I don't want to hang out at parties with you. But if you brag about your clients' successes on your newsletter, your emails, in your speeches or even over coffee, I'm impressed. Especially if who you're bragging about was in the same kind of pain as I was.

Now I am totally interested. You had me at 'My name is...'

Niche Dammit

Remember, when you're niched properly (go back to the chapter on this if you're not sure) then people will actually understand and be able to remember exactly who you help and what you help them do. Clarity is money in my world.

A Thousand Thank Yous

When you do get referrals, recognize them in some significant way. Nobody HAS to refer you or remember your name or even take the trouble of forwarding your information to anyone. They do so because they believe you can help their friend. Don't take it for granted.

Do Onto Others

This is a version of 'you scratch my back...' but in *Gentle* Marketing, it's done in authenticity and reciprocity. It's paying kindness forward, sharing resources and empowering your community and networks. When you're responsible for an acquaintance who you admire to get new clients, then all parties win. You win for having done a superb matchmaking job, while the referee and the referred win a valuable relationship.

So refer your little heart off, it can only get you more of the same. Remember to scope out businesses who serve a similar target and this referral game will net you even bigger results.

Plan It Sista!

When you actually have a cross referral program, you're telling ideal joint venture partners up front that you can actually provide them with a gift for thinking of your services to refer to first. This is *Gentle* Marketing because it's based on a gift and an invitation. It is based on trust between both parties and the essence of collaboration.

Come Clean

When you add a tagline to your email or to your social media profiles or even to your business card that says something like 'We LOVE referrals', it's a *Gentle* reminder to send business your way.

Forums R Us

Get onto social media forums and answer questions related to your specialty. I have a client who gets TONS of business from doing just that on Linkedin groups. With just 15 minutes a day's work, she's positioned herself as an expert in her industry and gotten several referrals a month from answering questions.

Referrals are as *Gentle* as you can get in Marketing.

The big thing that most businesses don't do properly is to follow up. What good is any marketing if you're going to ignore your leads? So please, don't forget to wine, dine and drop a line to your referrals.

Workbook

1. What ONE thing can you do to *Gently* ask your current clients for referrals?

_____

_____

_____

_____

_____

_____

2. Who is on your shortlist to cross refer with?

_____

_____

_____

_____

_____

_____

3. What kind of cross-referral fee or program can you offer to businesses who serve the same target as you?

_____

_____

_____

_____

_____

_____

4. What will you do to BRAG about a client regularly every month? (ie. Put in newsletter, send out emails, mention on radio interview etc.)

_____

_____

_____

_____

_____

_____

5. What social media forums do your future clients hang out in and what groups are asking questions you can answer on a regular basis?

_____

_____

_____

_____

_____

_____

"In order to succeed, your desire for success should be greater than your fear of failure."
Bill Cosby

9

Gentle Schmoozing:
How To Be(e) The Honey
To Your Clients

Networking (schmoozing) events are possibly the most critical places where you can practice *Gentle* Marketing. Remember my story about how I was accused of 'Attacking' a woman with a sales pitch at the beginning of my career? Well, the scene of that particular crime was—what else, a networking event.

So let me share a few secrets on how to turn networking into *Gentle* Schmoozing that will attract future clients.

The Terrified Schmoozer

I used to be a terrified networker–afraid of those milling crowds and round table breakfasts. How could a self-confident professional speaker extravert like me be afraid?

Through the years, the shift I made from "what can you give me" to "how can I serve your needs" has become a phenomenal change in the way I marketed my services. In other words, I *Gentled* my approach and have seen friendships and business referrals grow from a marketing technique that I used to hate and fear the most.

Here are some questions to ask yourself to see if you're a *Gentle* Marketer.

1. "Am I hanging out with my target clients?"

Jill (not her real name), a client of mine used to pay a fortune for a breakfast meeting at her own industry association. She didn't get a single client out of it over the three years that she attended religiously. Sure, she picked up industry trends and met many colleagues but she wasn't meeting any potential clients.

Once you've picked a solid niche target market, you need to be spending every dime and moment being in contact with them. Anything else is called education, not marketing.

2. **"Am I clear about exactly what benefit I deliver to my clients?"**

When you can't simply answer the question "and what do you do?" by concisely stating *what* you offer to *whom* about *which* problem, you can't expect people to refer others to you. They won't remember to pick out the essence of what you've said; therefore you'll have wasted your opportunity to connect with someone who needs your help. Remember what a Niching stickler I am!

3. **"What can I offer people I meet?"**

Whenever I now meet people, no matter where I meet them, I listen intently to what they're saying to see where the helping opportunity for me is. For example, a gentleman I met at a recent function told me he was looking into working as a strategist for a not-for-profit organization. Although he was neither in my target group currently, nor in need of my business services, I followed up and sent him the name of a person I'd met this year who did exactly what he was hoping to do. I now consider this gentleman a part of my network.

4. **"How do I become memorable to these people I'm meeting?"**

One thing I ask the people on my network is if they'd like to receive my E-zines. Provided they say yes, whether they're in my target market or not, they get a reminder of me once a month.

Another way I keep my network current is to send articles of interest to them randomly. The key thing is to continue to provide value to my network through a steady stream of kindnesses and referrals, never expecting anything in return.

5. "How does this help me get more business?"

It is the most integral part of *Gentle* Marketing. You are what you attract and what you attract is what you are. When you provide value, you are the recipient of similar value.

I have secured clients, speaking engagements and article placements through these techniques of networking. The terrorized networker I used to be is now one of the most relaxed, caring people in the room. (I no longer need antacids after networking)

I challenge you to try the same mental shift and attract business in the same way that those in the know are doing at this moment, somewhere in a networking luncheon right now.

Workbook

1. Identify at least 3 networking events your future clients schmooze at. If you can't find events where your CLIENT TYPE congregates, you haven't picked an accessible niche. Go back and pick another one!

_____

_____

_____

_____

_____

2. What kind of no-strings-attached value can you give to at least 3 people you meet at your next event?

_____

_____

_____

_____

_____

_____

_____

3. With which potential clients you've met while networking can you follow up and have coffee with. By when?

_____

_____

_____

_____

_____

_____

"More marriages might survive if the partners realized that sometimes the better comes after the worse."

Doug Larson

10

Getting Married
To Get More Clients

No, I'm not suggesting you actually go out and get married to another human being to get more clients! I'm only suggesting marriage to another business. And only temporarily.

What the heck am I talking about, you ask?

We live in the age of collaboration. All around us, one man (or woman) shows are becoming extinct and joint ventures have emerged as the new marketing tool to fill our practices.

For most of us, it's still a new experience to marry another business—whether for the duration of a co-promotion, an event or even a longer term joint venture project.

Marrying another business temporarily is a very *Gentle* way to get clients.

Your *temporary marriage* gives you:

- Potential custody of their children (their clients)

- Raises your profile so you can gain potential new kids (again-clients) of your own and through your collaboration

- Makes your business more attractive to a whole new population of people whose radar you never even blipped on (I don't know where to go with the kids analogy on this one)

A great example of a recent marriage I made was when a professional chef who catered to small businesses and I did a workshop together. She did the food demo and I did the marketing training. We both used our newsletters to promote the event to our databases. As a result of our marriage, we both got clients out of the workshop: I got coaching clients; she got other small business workshops to cook and serve at.

3 Top Reasons To Marry Gain More Ravers

If you have similar clients but don't compete directly for the same business, then you can mine each other's existing database and current client list to see if there's a match. Why shouldn't you offer your clients a tried and tested resource that complements what they hired *you* for?

1. 2 Heads Are Better Than Yours

Even if you're God's gift to your industry, when it comes to getting new clients, a collaborative effort is bound to yield more creativity and market relevance.

When I joint ventured on a proposal to a new client, we corrected each other's mistakes and came up with really creative new solutions to make our offering even better than it would've been had we worked in isolation.

2. Your Bra Isn't Supporting You Enough

When you only have yourself and your bra to depend on, your business can feel very isolating. I sit at my desk for a full 8 hours in my own home until I go to pick up my 3 year old and even then the conversation isn't scintillating at its best. If you're in the same boat, marrying another business temporarily allows you the support and interaction with another person who is exactly like you.

3. In Cheapness and In Health

When you marry another business temporarily, economies of scale can really work to a small business' advantage. Lump your powers to buy together and see how you can enhance your discounts and buying prowess.

The Mistakes To Avoid With Temporary Business Marriages

The Flip Side Of Marriage

Just like any marriage, there are potential pitfalls of partnering with another business for the purpose of getting new clients.

Here are some personal pet peeves to avoid when collaborating with another business (this is very similar to finding a real life marriage partner by the way!)

Not speaking the same language

If by "we'll connect soon" you mean tomorrow and they mean a week from now, this is a huge factor in how well the collaboration might go. I say scope out the first few interactions and bail quickly if you're not in synch.

Not setting expectation of collaboration at beginning

While you might love making new friends, you're in this partnership to ultimately make more money. Whether you're expecting more exposure, new leads, list access or cost sharing from your joint venture, clarify and quantify what each of you are expecting *before* you start the partnership. Also talk about contingencies of what happens if either party can't deliver those expectations. There's nothing worse than a wasted partnership that goes sour.

Not making a fair division of duties

I collaborated with a partner on an event where I agreed to doing most of the work and getting no cash rewards for the benefit of getting client leads for my coaching business. The unfairness of the division of duties, not to mention the lack of cash while I busted my chops to fill seats rankled deeply even though it was MY IDEA to do it that way. Since that experience, I've never offered to do anything more than my partner and never accepted anything less than equal profits.

Not making sure your brand characters mesh well together

If you're strictly George Clooney territory and you're doing a partnership with a business whose brand character is channelling Howard Stern, clearly there's a mismatch and any partnership will be potentially confusing and may be personally frustrating for all involved.

Once you've covered these ground rules, go ahead and join the bandwagon of collaboration. You'll see that one truly is the loneliest number—even in business.

Not putting it in writing

Even internet ministers know to get a signature on the marriage licence. How is it that businesses get married for events or cross referral programs without ever putting pen to paper. Detail especially the following on the agreement:

-Who will do what

-Who will get what (profits, benefits, placement on signage or flyer etc.)

-Who owns the list of participants for their database in events outside of the marriage with the same participants (remember – this is permission based marketing)

-How do you pay for costs?

-Who takes the money

-Length of marriage (haha, they should have this in real marriages from the start!)

These are just the basics that have bit me on the bum more than once so as long as you've got these covered, you're good.

Examples Of A Marriage:

- **Holding a co-event like a workshop or a networking event**: I did this several times with multiple partners ranging from personal chefs to other coaches. I love this one because it truly expands your reach.

- **Advertising together (shared links on each other's websites):** This is a form of affiliate marketing but without the money and the formality. I think if there's a real value businesses can add to each other, it's a real interesting thing to explore.

- **Sharing blogs and other content on each other's newsletters:** This one I've been doing for almost a decade. I've even had professional bloggers approach me and ask to be included in my website as content for the sole purpose of getting higher SEO for their articles.

- **Interviewing each other's business for content on your social media:** I've been interviewed by several other coaches and consultants. Having your own interview series is a great way to get and give exposure.

- **Buying something together to get discounts:** I created a Make Your Own Video day for my clients who are all coaches and consultants. Those who were too shy to make their own gathered together for a very reduced price where a videographer gave us a bulk rate to shoot and edit a 1 minute video for 10 of us.

What are some ideas you can come up with?

Go ahead, get married, I promise if you do it right, you'll become a polygamist in no time! After all, marriage is all about love and love is *Gentle*.

Workbook

1. What types of businesses serve the same CLIENT TYPE as you do?

_____

_____

_____

_____

_____

_____

2. Which of these have a similar brand character to yours?

_____

_____

_____

_____

_____

_____

3. What 3 different *Gentle* activities or events can you do by collaborating with another business to increase your visibility?

_____

_____

_____

_____

_____

_____

"All our dreams can come true, if we have the courage to pursue them."

Walt Disney

11

Putting It All Together: Make A Marketing Plan To Give Rocket Fuel To Your Biz

---

Why Have A Plan At All?

I f you're happy with the number of clients you have and the money you're earning, maybe how you've been doing things is perfectly fine and you should just keep doing them.

However, if you're like me, a *Gentle* Marketer who'd like to GROW your biz, then it's time to put strategy and structure into place and think ahead of the things you need to do to grow faster than you did last year.

What's your goal?

The first thing to figure out is how much did you make last year and from what streams of income? Then think about what you want to make the next 12 months and which streams do you want this to come from in what % chunks?

Your entire marketing plan depends on where you want to get business.

How to do a plan?

By now you have a clear target client and you know the activities you'll be doing around your target's hang out world to penetrate their attention.

Here are the simple-as-pie steps to making your plan:

1. Get a monthly calendar for the next 12 months.

That's pretty self-explanatory. You can do it electronically or paper. I'm ok with either as long as you're incorporating the marketing plans we talked about in this book.

2. Freaky Fridays

A practice I learned from my millionaire coach is to block off 1 day a week for doing marketing activities such as:

- calling leads you met networking,

- following up with people who've downloaded your free ebook,
- writing blogs
- sending your newsletters
- calling associations for public speaking
- crafting your speeches
- sending out thank you cards to joint venture or referral partners
- planning your presence at a trade show
- researching memberships for appropriate associations and so on

I've decided to make Friday my Marketing day so I've blocked off my entire year of Fridays

3. Pick 1-2 activities in each category your client's "Hangouts" to implement each month.

Ongoing Marketing Activities over and above the below list:

- Attend monthly meetings at 3 core associations: ewomen networks, COW and WIBN or PFW depending on the event and month
- Send newsletter to database every week
- Send thank you cards to associations and clients who work with me

January:

- Hold a Planning workshop in conjunction with PFW and TWE
- Get 1 speaking engagement at the Women In Biz Networks

February:

- Organize a workshop about How to Get New Clients
- Do a list building joint venture with another coach

March

- Call 5 networking leads to follow up
- Have coffee with 5 other new leads

April

- Call 5 associations for speaking opportunities
- Speak at the Diva Girl Conference

May

- Become a speaker at and have a booth at the PFW conference
- Have a booth at the WIBN conference

June

- Become a speaker and have a booth at the COW conference
- Hold a VIP strategy day for new potential clients

And so on.

4. Put details to it

Now that you've got the gist of what type of activity you'll be doing and in what month, you need to put a plan in place to get the exact date, time and cost nailed down.

Also, if you're planning ie/ getting a speaking engagement during a certain month, the lead time might be as long as a year. So add that to your considerations and keep in mind your plan can (and should be) flexible.

A plan is the culmination of everything you know about how to get clients.

So put one in place and get in front of people who need you. Intercept them with your messaging over and over and over again until you carve out that space in their mind for being the only game in town for your expertise.

Workbook

1. How much did your business earn last year?

_____

_____

_____

_____

_____

_____

2. What streams of income made up that revenue? (ie. 1/3 came from coaching, 1/3 from consulting and 1/3 from book sales etc.)

_____

_____

_____

_____

_____

_____

3. What would you like to earn in the next 12 months?

_____

_____

_____

_____

_____

_____

4. What streams will make up your projected income
    in the next 12 months?

_____

_____

_____

_____

_____

_____

5. Your dedicated Marketing Day(your version of my
    Freaky Friday) will be?

_____

_____

_____

_____

_____

_____

6. What will be the ongoing marketing activities you'll do all year?

Your marketing activities in January

_____

Your marketing activities in February

_____

Your marketing activities in March

_____

Your marketing activities in April

_____

Your marketing activities in May

_____

Your marketing activities in June

_____

Your marketing activities in July

_____

Your marketing activities in August

_____

Your marketing activities in September

_____

Your marketing activities in October

_____

Your marketing activities in November

_____

Your marketing activities in December

_____

7.   What can get in the way of you implementing your plan?

_____

_____

_____

_____

_____

_____

_____

8. What resources do you have to get over that barrier?

_____

_____

_____

_____

_____

_____

"I am not a has-been. I am a will be."

Lauren Bacall

12

Too Chicken To Succeed

I f you've actually read this book past the first chapter, now you've seen the big bad world of marketing for the simple formula that it is.

Gentle Marketing really is all based on who you are and how well you can communicate how you can help people in a meaningful way.

You don't need to run after people. You don't need to make cold calls. You don't need to spend a fortune.

All you need is to be clear, authentic, strategic and different than everyone else who is doing the same thing as you.

Given how easy it is to market your business successfully to make big bucks, I thought I'd address the beast of the fear of success as part of this book.

I'm Afraid I'll Be Too Successful

A few nights ago at a small business networking meeting, a simple question was asked of the audience—

"What is your biggest pain point?"

Unanimously everyone agreed it wasn't having enough clients.

That sounds like a no brainer answer right?

Unfortunately in my practice of helping small businesses grow their client base, I run into a lot of people who are on some level afraid of actually succeeding.

Are You Worried That...

1. **"Things will change"**: The fear of change is the deepest and oldest fear of all man and woman kind. It's a big one to get over.

2. **"I'll have to spend less time with family and on myself "**: When success in business equals failure as a mom, daughter or spouse, people are often guilt ridden and find it tough to make a decision to do things to get more clients.

3. **"I'll have to do some things I hate (sales and marketing)":** Most small business owners love what they do but hate selling it. On some level, they know when they decide to get more clients, it means they'll inevitably have to market and sell more than they are right now.

4. **"Wanting too much money is greedy":** In a lot of subconscious small business owners' minds lies the thought that if things aren't too bad for them right now, why rock the boat? They think that to want more money,more clients and to want to play a bigger game is just plain greedy. Greed is not an attractive trait.

5. **"My friends and loved ones will think I'm a big shot":** Who would want anything if it meant estrangementand ruined relationships with loved ones? Who would pursue something that could cause their social circles to reject them?

Light at the end of the tunnel

- **Examine the root of the belief:** what happened or who were you surrounded by who kept reinforcing this limiting belief that change is bad or money is evil? If the belief comes from a childhood trauma and is preventing youfrom going forward, you might want to consider therapy to support you.

- **Surround yourself with successful people:** We've all heard that you are the average of the 5 people you hang around with. Change your posse to start changingyour mind!
- **Talk to the people who matter about your fears.** Most often, you'll see that the fears are groundless and that fear is just another mind trick self-delusion to keep you inactive.

Workbook

1. What are some of your specific fears around succeeding?

_____

_____

_____

_____

_____

_____

2. What evidence exists that your fear may not be true?

_____

_____

_____

_____

_____

_____

3. Who can you share your fears with who have built a successful business?

_____

_____

_____

_____

_____

_____

4. What's at stake if you don't address this?

_____

_____

_____

_____

_____

_____

5.   What is ONE thing you can do to overcome the biggest of your fears?

_____

_____

_____

_____

_____

_____

"Think twice before you speak, because your words and influence will plant the seed of either success or failure in the mind of another."

Napoleon Hill

13

Wow That Crowd-How To Gently Public Speak To Get Clients

P ublic Speaking is yet another way to *Gently* get clients. It's a really powerful marketing technique because it not only positions you as an expert in front of your bulls eye target client but also allows you to help and connect with large groups of people at one time.

My first public speaking experience was definitely NOT *Gentle*. In my 8th grade French class, I was doing my utmost to explain the mating habits of a praying mantis in French (they eat their partner once done with them!)

to a class room of English-speaking pre-teens. Everyone ignored me. I then stopped everyone in their tracks by starting to draw the actual mating process on the board and illustrating the eating that ensued thereafter. I managed to penetrate the teenage haze and got a few raised eyebrows that day. I haven't stopped wanting to arrest people in their tracks when I speak since then.

To *Gentle* your approach while public speaking, make sure it's all in service to your target clients. Remember, it's not about you, it's about THEM...

Here are some tips on how to achieve Gold speaker status while using public speaking to actually get clients.

What's The Audience's Pain?

Why are the people in those seats? What pain can you help them with today? With me, it's usually about getting more clients and figuring out a marketing plan to get there.

What's Your Solution?

There are a million ways to help the same problem but your audience is interested in finding out what you did in the past to help clients with similar pain and what their results were. If you tell interesting and relevant stories about how you helped another client with the same pain and all the wonderful outcomes of your actions, you give people a chance to find out how they can also benefit from your help.

Entertain Me

If you provide value but don't entertain people in some way–then you're missing the entire reason why people came to see you talk and not picked up a book. Audiences want to connect with you as a human, they want to hear personal stories and they want to be inspired and amused.

The shortest way to anybody's heart is to make them smile or even better to make them laugh. Even if you're not a comedian or an entertainer, tell a story of your past that made you smile. Make sure to link it to the audience pain and your solution. Then voila–you have a captivated audience!

Start With a Bang!

The biggest impression I know how to make when I speak is to tell a phoenix rising story that's as personal and painful as it can get. The caveat here is that it has to relate to the topic of the talk. You don't want to talk about your painful divorce at a fertilizer's convention. On second thought, maybe you do...

During my "*Attract not Attack: A Gentle Way to Get Clients*" seminar, I tell the humiliating story of how my first networking event ended up in a fiasco of a woman telling me that she felt 'attacked' by my sales pitch (which you already read about earlier). Upon hearing of my angst and the tools that I used to turn it around for my business, you can be sure that the audience was primed to hear more. Personal stories engage, connect and make you more accessible. It tells people that just like everyone in the audience, you make mistakes too.

Give It All Away

I'm a proponent of the school of 'giving it all away'. This means, tell everyone the best of everything you know for free. Don't hold back the better 'stuff' for paying clients. In my experience when people get amazing value from your content, they're going to be even more jazzed about working one on one with you.

Leaving The Offer On The Table

Most small business owners I meet who do any public speaking are missing this strategic opportunity of getting new clients. They don't make an offer from the stage. This offer, of course, can be an invitation to sign up for a complimentary session or a newsletter or even to actually buy. When a speaker who has a captive audience can't or won't use the opportunity to connect further with a strong and specific offer from the stage, I call that a darn shame.

Free or Paid?

I have gotten most of my clients from free speaking and have made it part of my marketing strategy to speak at association chapter meetings, national organization webinars and annual general meetings or conferences for FREE. I won't refuse the money if offered but I don't have a hang up about it since I get so many clients out of doing it free or paid. The only condition I have if it's free is that it's in front of my target clients. If it's not, then I ask for money.

Try And Try Again

When I can't get into an event as a speaker, I keep the relationship fresh until I apply for the upcoming year's event. In addition, I offer some other way to stay relevant and valuable. For example, I offer free blog or vlog (video blog) content for their publication. Or I do free conference coaching. *Gentle* marketing is about providing value and building long term relationships.

Getting The Gigs

How do I get the speaking jobs? I first start with understanding where my potential clients are hanging out. I research the associations and events or trade shows they attend.

If I don't know where they're hanging out, I simply ask my target what professional meetings or conferences they've attended in the last 12 months.

The next step is to call the association or organization and ask *"Who is the person who decides on bringing in speakers for your meetings and conferences"*

Once I find the person who will hire me (or vet me), I have a short chat about my speaking topic (which should ALWAYS be about their members' pain points) and follow up by sending them an email with a speaking summary that includes a punchy bio and next steps.

The *Gentle* Follow Up

If there's interest while you're chatting, then you ask the organizers *"when would it be appropriate for me to follow up with you?"* This is *Gentle* Marketing at its best because you're asking for their permission and timeline to follow up.

In addition, something I've recently started to do is to add a video of a vlog (video blog) to my proposal to give them an experience of me. This has really been increasing my success rate at getting accepted as a speaker.

Here's an example of an email I sent after speaking to the association coordinator who does the speaker hiring:

Mary,

Thanks for the nice chat and for the opportunity to speak at the Malton Hills Chamber. Here's a video of me to give you an idea of who I am: *http://www.youtube. com/watch?v=TmFonD2afbl*

Here's my speaking topic:

Gentle Marketing: How To Gently Attract Loads Of Customers

Do you want to learn how to attract NEW customers instead of chasing after them with canned marketing campaigns? How do you stand out and tell clients that you can help them?

In this informative and action packed seminar, you will learn:

- The number one reason why businesses confuse potential customers and MISS the opportunity(yikes!)

- How to get into your client's world and get THEM to ask to work with you

- Discover the business changing secret to *Gently* attracting clients instead of chasing them

A bio of me:

Chala Dincoy is the CEO and Founder of Coachtactics, www.coachtactics.com. She's a brand marketing expert who helps small businesses feel like a NATIONAL BRAND (without paying the big bucks!)

In her former life, Chala was an award winning marketer at companies such as Pepsi, Pizza Hut, Frito Lay, Diageo, Playtex and BIC Inc for 20 years. Now, she's the author of Gentle Marketing, a speaker featured on

Rogers TV and a certified business coach, who speaks about turning your brand into rocket fuel so you get more clients!

Chala dishes out big advice that's to the point, cuts your costs and helps make your brand look like a ROCK STAR to customers!

I look forward to connecting after April 8th!

Regards,

Chala

Sex Sells

A sexy title is everything when you're trying to sell your talk. You say you're not a copy writer? No worries, neither am I. Here are some tips and tricks I've picked up in my long and illustrious marketing career:

- I copy the magazine cover headlines. (ex. *Turn Your Boyfriend Into Your Slave* becomes *Turn Your Audience Into Raving Clients*)
- I look at my competitors' keynote titles and turn them on their ear (ex. *90-Minute Marketing Plans That Get Results*" becomes *"The Un-Marketing Plan...a different look at how to stand out"*
- I make it rhyme (ex. *Attract not Attack, Wow that Crowd*)

- I make it controversial (ex. *Fire Your Sales Staff: SEO at work*)
- I quote their pain (ex. *Exhausted and Overwhelmed About Marketing Your Biz?*)

Helping large groups of your target audience is a dream come true for many of my clients. You don't have to be Oprah, you don't have to be slick. Just be yourself. If big crowds scare you, start with your living room and friends. Just try it.

Public Speaking can be so powerful, that it can be the single marketing strategy that you use to build your entire business.

So I beg you as a frequent audience member to please use these tips at your next talk so that you can *Gently* wow me and everyone that I'm sitting next to as you quietly fill your practice.

Workbook

1. What meetings, events and conferences are your target clients attending?

_____

_____

_____

_____

_____

_____

2. What is your target client's pain point?

_____

_____

_____

_____

_____

_____

3. What is a sexy title for your main keynote that relates to their pain point?

_____

_____

_____

_____

_____

_____

4. What will be the 3 things your audience will get out of hearing you talk (build this into your summary)

_____

_____

_____

_____

_____

_____

5. What will you offer at the end of your talk as a natural next step to help your audience and build your business?

_____

_____

_____

_____

_____

_____

"The chief cause of failure and unhappiness is trading what you want most for what you want right now."

Zig Ziglar

14

Last Word

I hope this book about *Gentle* Marketing has been thought (and giggle) provoking for you. As a small business I know you are bombarded by opinions on what to do and how to do it on a daily basis.

Why is this book any different?

Because it's the culmination of a deep need that I've seen and felt in small business owners. And that need is NOT going away. I know how to help and I can't die with the answers in me. I see it in the faces of business owners everyday...

The need to attract without subterfuge.

The ability to cultivate a fan base quickly and effortlessly.

The desire to succeed without losing one's self-respect.

Here are some final thoughts about helping you, the small business owner become an unqualified success.

Follow Your Dreams

In a recent talk I gave about following your dreams to leave your day job and to launch your own business, I had a young man in the audience point out that his mother had never been there for him because of her business and that he had suffered greatly for it. He accused me of trying to convince other moms to do the same and to abandon their children in sacrifice of their dreams. Everyone in the audience (including me) was taken aback and kind of speechless.

Realizing your dreams is entirely possible while having a balanced family life. I'm living proof of it. It's not easy and it's not overnight but making money at what your heart desires is completely do-able. You need a plan, you need clarity and you need help.

A Helping Hand

You can't do it alone.

Why?

Because you simply don't know what you don't know.

Why should you have to lose time figuring it out? I am proud to say that before I left my daytime job, even as I had no clients to support my coaching practice, I gave my last paycheque over to my coach. As a result, I now have a thriving and enjoyable practice.

Could I have done it alone or would I have been part of that International Coaching Federation statistic that states that the median annual income for a certified coach is below poverty level? Who can know?

My point is, the fastest and most enjoyable route to getting more business is to learn from someone who has dedicated their life to people like you succeeding.

All You Need Is Love

I sound like an old jukebox here with these song titles but love is what I give to my clients and community each and every day.

Yes, it's corny and yet it's trite but there it is.

Every day, I get up and think about how I'm going to help my clients or what blog topic would be most relevant to their pain. Each minute, I think about how I can make my material more fun and digestible and useful.

One of my favourite authors Robert Holden says *"if your definition of success doesn't have the word love in it, then you need to get a different definition"* and I couldn't agree more.

Gentle Is As Gentle Does

When I was 20, an ex once likened me to a 'brillo pad' because of my abrasive personality. He was a kind soul, wasn't he? Nevertheless, I am the last thing from a shy retiring sort of personality. How is it then that I'm touting a concept called *Gentle* Marketing? A concept that's based on attraction and not aggression?

Well, I've learned the hard way that aggression for anything in life doesn't work.

Being strategic, being clear and being strong about what I stand for have attracted me many clients and will continue to do so in the coming years.

What I Want For You

In coaching there's something called 'wanting for'. This is something we say to acknowledge and motivate our clients about a goal they have. The technique is to take what they want for themselves and exaggerate it so that it's even better than they could ever dream of. The effect is supposed to be so powerful that it leaves a client feeling like they can climb a mountain barefoot!

So what *I* want for you all is never to feel dirty or uncomfortable about marketing yourselves ever again.

I want you to know exactly who you help and how you help them. I want you to be able to instinctively and without hesitation tell people what you do for a living and have them walk away with smiles and nods.

Above all, I want you to *Gently* attract so many of the kinds of clients and business partners to you that you no longer have to even think about marketing yourself ever again.

15

Acknowledgements

I'd like to thank the academy, my fans and God as the speech goes.

Seriously, it does take a village and I'd like to thank my bossy diva coach Kim Duke for bossing this idea that was already in my head into an actual printed book. She's a true coach in every sense of the word. She guides, kicks butt when needed, advises and corrects. I love her.

To my husband who always loved and supported me even when times were lean and he must've been just as scared as I was at the start. He should be cloned for all women entrepreneurs (but he's all mine and I won't share ha!)

To my family, we might be small but we rock. I love you guys.

To my clients who teach me something valuable every day. I couldn't have written this without them.

To my community of friends and community leaders who support me in my exciting career, they continue to inspire me every day.

To Logan, the love of my life—I want to make the world a better place for you pal, and this is how I'm bettering this corner of my world. Hope you like the results when you grow up.

To Wayne Dyer, you have always inspired me and were better than a hundred therapists. See you on the cruise soon!

16

Resources

These books have shaped and guided my thoughts for many years. Pick them up and see how they help you!

Success Intelligence, Robert Holden PHD

UnMarketing: Stop Marketing. Start Engaging, Scott Stratten

Permission Marketing : Turning Strangers Into Friends And Friends Into Customers – Seth Godin

How To Win Friends and Influence People – Dale Carnegie

Enchantment: The Art of Changing Hearts, Minds, and Actions – Guy Kawasaki

POP!: Create the Perfect Pitch, Title, and Tagline for Anything – Sam Horn

Why We Buy: The Science of Shopping – Paco Underhill

The Power of Intention Learning to Co-create Your World Your Way - Dr. Wayne W. Dyer

You Can Heal Your Life - Louise Hay

32412666R00098